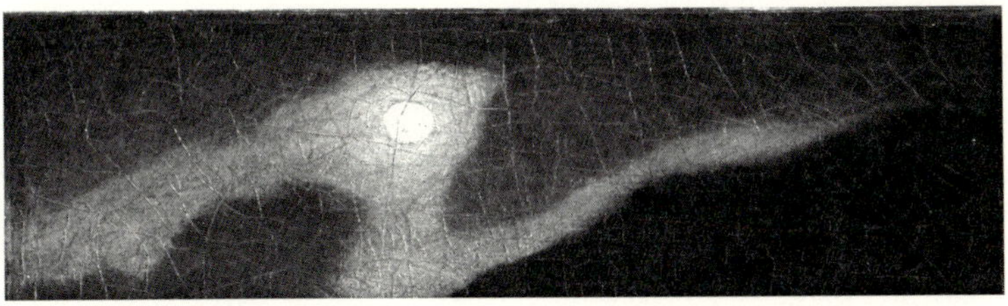

GREEN MIDNIGHT

5/5/2021

For Sam,

poems

STUART BARTOW

DOS MADRES

2018

DOS MADRES PRESS INC.
P.O.Box 294, Loveland, Ohio 45140
www.dosmadres.com editor@dosmadres.com

Dos Madres is dedicated to the belief that the small press is essential to the vitality of contemporary literature as a carrier of the new voice, as well as the older, sometimes forgotten voices of the past. And in an ever more virtual world, to the creation of fine books pleasing to the eye and hand.

Dos Madres is named in honor of Vera Murphy and Libbie Hughes, the "Dos Madres" whose contributions have made this press possible.

Dos Madres Press, Inc. is an Ohio Not For Profit Corporation and a 501 (c) (3) qualified public charity. Contributions are tax deductible.

Executive Editor: Robert J. Murphy

Illustration & Book Design: Elizabeth H. Murphy
www.illusionstudios.net

Typeset in Adobe Garamond Pro & Charlemagne Std
ISBN 978-1-948017-12-1
Library of Congress Control Number: 2018937481

First Edition

Published by Dos Madres Press, Inc.

ACKNOWLEDGEMENTS

Verse Daily: "Syrens"
Misfit Magazine: "Albany"; "After Hearing Bobby Knight Rail"; "Cat Women on Mars"
Pine Hills Review: "Green Bottle"
Stillwater Review: "Page Pond"
La Presa: "Do Not Open After Dusk"; "Long Time"; "Hearts"; "Ghost Orchestras"
The Arabesques Review: "Invasion"; "Teaching Tennyson and Yeats to Veterans"; "Swifts at Dusk"; "Merlins"; "Orb Weavers"; "Citizen Sparrows"; "Marooned"
Chronogram: "Shell"
Stone Walls II: "Orb Weavers"
Birchsong: "On the Porch Roof After a Snowstorm"
Woodstock Poetry Society: "Calling the Muse"; "Blackboard"; "Orpheus"

Cover Art:
Ryder, Albert Pinkham, *Moonlit Cove*, 1880s, Oil on Canvas, 14 1/8 x 17 1/8 in.; 35.8775 x 43.4975 cm.
The Phillips Collection, Washington, D. C. Acquired 1924

Author Photo: Dan Wilcox

For BLU, my consort, always

TABLE OF CONTENTS

I GREEN BOTTLE

II THE WIND AT 4 A.M.

III REDWINGS

GREEN MIDNIGHT

In the green midnight by the nightingale's northern limit
. . . time doesn't exist. Just the nightingale's voice, those raw
ringing notes that whet the night sky's bright scythe.

Tomas Transtromer, translated by Patty Crane

✧ I ✧

GREEN BOTTLE

CALLING THE MUSE

I'm superstitious about calling the muse,
don't want her to get the wrong
idea. Who needs to make
a poem every day
when one has real work to do,
shoveling snow, washing dishes,
drinking? And doesn't she
have other things to do, like
tend to her other loves,
that mountain in Greece, the wind
at 4 a.m., the Milky Way?
Making visitation to those lost souls
who need to write something
about love, or despair,
or loneliness. I don't want her
to know I want her, need
her close. After all, if I call
too often, she may tire of me,
even though I've memorized
her number: (099) 999-9999.

VAMPIRES IN THE ATOMIC AGE

Vampires are all the rage
in this age of climate change. They
cast no shadows anywhere,
in the mirror no one there.
They are among us only
as appearances. Maybe they
are the sole ones who believe
in the soul, for theirs are astray,
absent from their bodies
which do not age. Maybe
without a soul one cannot die
or love, whatever that may be.
But they do crave
the beautiful, at least their blood.
They do not need
insurance. They do not dream
of gods or money, only
of blood, old music,
recordings that crackle
like echoes from long
demolished dance halls.
They are captains of
the shapeless vessel of night.

CAT WOMEN ON MARS

or was it the moon? That fifties black and white
made in a few weeks
for a few thousand, with starlets
and hunks, scripted by alcoholics,
wound up on midnight TV
where adolescent boys like me
absorbed this weird idea
of sexual identity staged as fantasy
or visa versa. An old story.
Odysseus and his men strand
their phallic ship
on an alien island inhabited
by magical females.
But never forget, fellow dreamers,
beware of strange stars: that lost crew
as often as not failed to crash on Venus,
landed on cannibal wildernesses,
bleak places, cyclopes.

ON THE PORCH ROOF
AFTER A SNOWSTORM

I scan the town where wisps of smoke
vanish from chimneys here and there.
The rumble of plow trucks has yet to reach
the stillness. As I begin to shovel
I recall the ancient Chinese believed
poets were divine beings
sentenced to toil on earth
for some trespass in heaven. The snow
cascades off the roof,
showers made not
by a passing comet, but by
my labor. Something draws me
to look up. The wind has erased
the clouds. Stars return. I feel
a twinge of homesickness. Home
is thousands of light years away
and the only way to escape
this happy doom
is to fall.

ALBANY

On this overcast March day on the corner
of Sherman and Quail, a raven is quacking.
Yes, quacking. I can't locate her. There's
a black plastic bag stuck in a tree.
It's not her. I imagine no one knows
a raven is laughing at us on this street
where I read the stores: African Hair Braiding,
Adam's Barber Shop, Mr. Stuff, Yemen
Grocery and Deli, Albany Boxing,
Caribbean Produce and Variety,
Beryl's Beauty Salon, Up-Top Fragrance
and Lingerie. Some men are playing hip
hop loud. The raven loves this music.
I carry a book of poems, feeling good
in the wind in an alien land.

GREEN BOTTLE

The green bottle I began to dislodge
then stopped, seeing an ant colony
inside, so left them to their toil,
wondering if they see the glass symmetry
as just a random object from the sky,
and considered how right they'd be,
unmoved by reckless divinities
who might prowl earth and sky and,
like curious, meddlesome children,
marvel at the strange uses we make
of their wreckage, their genius.

SYRENS

Some say they were twain, yet this is hearsay.
All who might've seen these sisters veered astray,
shipwrecked then eaten. No one escaped
but one who sailed past screaming, mast-bound liar,

and a poet who dreamed them with his lyre.
Odysseus never once claimed sight
of these winged women, never made count,
told of their wings, talons, throats. No doubt

the enchantment of their song, their sound
was unlike any birds', but a human choir,
a girl-group that knew yearning without hope.
Avian, after all, syrinx inside their throats

to sing in many notes and warble heartache
multi-voiced, a gift, a curse we can't imitate.

AFTER HEARING BOBBY KNIGHT RAIL AGAINST BASEBALL PLAYERS WHO POINT TO HEAVEN AND CROSS THEMSELVES AFTER HOMERING OR SAVING A GAME

Jesus does not wear a Marlins cap,
perched in the bleachers as he guides
Giancarlo Stanton's homerun over the wall
munching on popcorn, nor make miracles
for the Rays because they ceased being devils.
But the gods do interfere. Ares
and Aphrodite secretly date
at Dodgers Stadium, Zeus hates
domes and Astroturf, the Mariners
are kept submerged by Poseidon,
Pallas Athena has a love-hate passion
for the Red Sox, Hermes tinkers
with the White Sox for not wearing their
sox white and winged, and Circe
has hexed men into Cubs, cursed
to fail year after year. Persephone emerges
each spring in her cotton dress,
drifting unseen through the gates to witness
the fresh young men. Apollo
roots for those named for the singers of the sky,
Cardinals, Blue Jays, Orioles.
For the Giants in San Francisco,
Aeoleus wanders where he likes.
And Hephaestus peers
over his forge and through the clouds,
Pirates the team he bellows and shouts.

But I wonder, sometimes, about the Adversary
in his Yankees t-shirt with the twenty seven
titles, Beelzebub whispering
into their third base coach's ear;
on the bench of the vaunted team,
Mephistopheles managing, no, guiding, affairs.

DROPPING OUT OF THE VISUAL POETRY WORKSHOP AT THE RENSSELAERVILLE LIBRARY

The clouds here turn only into people's faces.

The mountains cause you to dream fitfully.

In this town singing occurs only at dawn.

The biggest store is a bicycle shop open only on Wednesdays.

Late for the free-write, snatching paper from the garbage, I got only a few images down before it ended, and glanced up to see the room shrunken close with poets. Surrendering my chair, I fled upstairs where I found Frank O'Connor's *Collected Stories*, and read *The Lady of the Sages*. Deirdre Costello, grey-eyed school teacher, bored in a boring town, in love with an imaginary bad boy. She's horrified to learn that the scandalous lawyer she yearns after is not naughty at all, but actually quite ordinary, which destroys the spell.

I gaze out the library window where the early spring snow is swirling, and where, right at the back steps, a doe is grazing. The library is under a spell (falling from the sky) that the poets have conjured by their basement toil. We are in a snow dome of their creation, but they are not finished. I know the way out, the way to the door. I am confident that I can save myself before the enclosure is sealed, perhaps forever. But the wind is rising, the snow, heavier.

WITHOUT THE STARS

Without the stars there'd be no us.
Can intention hide in the vacant rifts?
Remnants of ancient stardust,

made constellations by wanderlust,
can cause be within cause like something wished?
Without the stars there'd be no us.

What are those glowing shapes to lightning bugs,
to moths, whales, all the fish,
remnants of ancient stardust

that dwell also in the lonely slug
who cannot see the stars that dance and drift.
Without the stars there'd be no us.

We can watch the stellar gusts,
can rue the meteors we've missed,
still not forgetting we are stardust

that somehow makes us know the stars enough,
the knowing enough to conjure bliss.
We know without the stars there would not be us,
all of us made of ancient stardust.

ORPHEUS

All the night's fleeting drama once we wake
crumbles into a vortex we can't remake

as if we were created never to look back.
To resurrect Eurydice, such

hard work, poetry readings to the dead,
harp recitals in vacant catacombs,

hexameters for shades, Sapphic stanzas
rehearsed to shadows, and soothing tones

for junkyard dogs. Eventually he reached
the undiscovered country

on no map, that sends magnetic fields
to pull us back and forth like geese.

He found the stone couple in their inverted
penthouse, charmed them enough to return

his bride, though it was plain to see,
even through all the murk,

they would never surface alive. No one can
not glance back. They knew no living mortal

could bring so much quickness out their portal.
He tried, got to see her outstretched arms

evaporate, what we see when morning light
obliterates the stars. It happens every day.

INVASION

Back before the wood across the road was cleared,
the fields bulldozed and housed over,
the last farm blinked out and disappeared
under pavement, lightning bugs roamed summer
nights. Back when the Milky Way pavilioned
the sky before street lights made us forget,
I would gaze in wonder
and some random dread.

Abandonment, absence of angels,
a sense we could not read the book of spells
the wind had splayed open before us
before our war against the weeds.
Today, paralyzed in summer
traffic, they come in legions, tiny parachutes,
dandelion storm.

ORB WEAVERS

Each night the orb weaver spins a new web.
Each night stars arrive whether or not
we see them. When we fall into sleep our minds
weave our day's strands into dramas unrehearsed.

Pluto's mountains seem to be dreamt. The universe,
with its dark matter, dark energy, is comprised
mostly of what we cannot see. Why
does the orb weaver toil so? Why
can't she simply sleep and make repairs
as needed? The mind wends in restless orbits,
traces like rising mist, old dread.
By morning, near my back porch, I'll greet her,
move past carefully, and not break a thread.

MAROONED

Pretending to be a great explorer
I found the wreck alone, tilting between
sandbars, then showed her to *Her*, the secret
ours. The decaying boat seemed
possessed, a ghost ship that strayed each
night, to be found in different places
each time we strolled the beach. The boat
became our haven, summer hideaway,
the helm intact, sea restless out the portholes.
Donna, where are you marooned,
or stranded by ocean that churns and rolls?
Did I imagine you those afternoons?
One day we wandered out to an empty beach,
the ship swept out to sea.

TEACHING TENNYSON AND YEATS TO VETERANS

They like The Charge, the doomed flash.
They get the tragic mess that's made
by obeying bad orders. They understand
the communality of courage, know
accidents, chance, luck, perhaps the dreamish
sense that the world of peace is unreal,
suffer daily the ache of survivors.
To fight over a beautiful woman? For
them it's not a face that launched a thousand
ships to burn the towers of Troy.
It's not about vanity or sex.
It's battlefield blunder they've lived and lost.
It's surviving the nightmare machine
oiled by old men. It's passing the test.

THE MERMAID

Statuette, foot tall with sweeping tail,
holding a bowl that should have carried seashells,
instead her head in a platter like John
the Baptist, stood outside
the defunct gas company
amidst scattered ruins of other statuary.

I considered pillage, hauling
her onto the back of my truck,
but scruples or superstition stopped me.
Still, she needed rescue, needed to adorn
the ruins of my garden, her head restored.
Too late. When I returned
she was gone. Some other treasured her
curves, her strange smile so demure.

LOVING ELSA

When I first saw the mad scientists, Drs.
Pretorius and Frankenstein, unveil her bewildered
feline gaze, her beehive streaked with gray, her
slender, unsteady gait, something moved
in my thirteen-year-old body and wild mind.
Beneath her bandages, both wedding dress
and swaddling clothes, she was female in all
her inscrutable purity, and a monster.
Did the crush begin when they unraveled her?
The wicked goal to make a race of gods
collapsed. She wanted Frankenstein, not his creature.
The scene replays, again the tower falls.
The bolt ignites the kite
to wake the bride again.

✧ II ✧

THE WIND AT 4 A.M.

LUST

Love or lust, she declared from the back
of the classroom, what difference does it make?
And, after all, isn't it only words, parsing.
That back road I often travel, that
fist of sparrows between the fields, their

sister or mate gliding too low, car-clipped,
stranded in the road's middle, still singing
to her flock as they fretted around her,
scattering back to the bushes between
passing pickup trucks, then returning,
trying to levitate their love through song
that their urging might make miracle,
and I thought, maybe, that's the difference.

GHOST ORCHESTRAS

In an isolated old farmhouse in Cambridge,
New York, out of the blue, a big band number
from a vanished radio show
would start to play at odd times in the kitchen
or other rooms, the broadcast sometimes faint,
sometimes clear. Armstrong or one
of the Dorseys, Shaw or Ellington,
the voiceless croon of Glen Miller's band.

Imagine a woman for whom the radio
was companion, and her solitude so deep,
and the music so loved, it imprinted
on the ballroom ceiling
of the night sky. That music
a constellation sending out radio waves,
an echo in search of its home.

DO NOT OPEN AFTER DUSK

said the sign on the steel back door
of the coffee shop. I'd been on that side street
at dusk and thought nothing magical there
except maybe a bit more strange than other
streets. Of course the sign was about fear
but I always like to open portals
to see dusk, to go out into
space and time between

like William Blake, who,
in sunrise and set,
saw a golden chorus singing.
I, too, have dreamt
of one day opening that door

to meet something on the other side, to answer
that call, like Oisin who returned
through the only door back
which is always the wrong door
because time is also a place
that lasts only as memory, and his week
or month in twilight was three hundred years.

Yet I, too, can't resist, just a peek,
and have whimsied into the strange, last light,
that first step, after which
the door behind doesn't lock
but disappears.

THE GEMINIDS

Hiked to the hill behind my house,
the dead factory and the town's glow
near midnight when dark obliterates made light,
stood upon that height,
a watcher of the skies.
Had to yank my spaniel's leash—
she trembled for fear of something
we could not see, a yowling
fishercat whose cries
wandered disembodied.

Stars streaked across the sky
near and faint, and I the one, the only
witness of this scene
wondered about all those in the dream
of their winter homes, none awake.
Whether the falling stars had any magic to invade
their sleep, or if, like hibernating beetles,
they missed the streaming meteors
that arced across the sky.

CAROLINA WRENS

do not migrate.
They are moving farther north.
They thrive when winters are mild
but heavy snow and cold
can devastate them. They like
woodland thickets, ravines,
rocky slopes covered with brush.
Their eggs, usually five, are white
with brown spots. Rich brown above,
buff or yellow chests, these wrens
have a distinct white line
above and behind their eyes.
Their nests are domed, feather-lined,
made of sticks with an entrance at the side.
Their nests are built in stone walls,
hollow tree stumps, tin cans,
birdhouses, mailboxes and even
coat pockets on clotheslines.
This February morning you stop me
in my tracks with a tweedle
I've never heard before, and light
near, in the berry bush hedgerow,
and I think how vulnerable
yet strong we are, while you let me
get a good close look at you, as though
you dropped by to give me this poem.

CONVERSATION WITH MY HOUSE

You are a she, a little ship
coursing through time and space
though I've yet to speak your name
because the right one hasn't reached my lips.

I've told you in your dreams.

Tell me again. My dreams blur and lose
their form. Is there sound in dreams?

There are all the clues.

There is an encyclopedia of lost clues.

*I want you here forever, long
as you live. I want you
to die here, inside me.*

But your name, *Hidden in Town,
Woman Who Cloaks—*
the name begins to shape
but as sleep clears, evaporates
and makes me feel as though
something profound eludes my days
and nights. In blurry dreams
I search your name
in a crumbling book, on a wall, or screen,
a scrap of paper, and as I float
attic-bound, mind

or spirit or whatever it is in me
wanders to the roof
then beyond
unnamed.

ANTS

Used to wage war
pretending they were alien armies,
blacks and reds in combat.
I'd find their mounds and plant firecrackers,
delight in the chaos. Years later
I found Thoreau, his Iliad of ants.
Now I marvel even more: their
varieties, colonies, wars, labyrinths,
queens, doomed princes, their Borg-
like tenacity, how they hold the earth
together; unlike us, envious, ruinous
as Homer's gods, giants the ants
regard like storms.

WATCHERS

Lightning bugs are thick in the marsh
behind my house so sometimes on June nights
I'll trek down the road
to see their fracturing green constellations
just to remind myself of something.
In the daytime they're mere beetles,
sleek and bronze, nondescript,
like us. But when we sleep
we, too, are at the other side
of ourselves. We might be emitting
a spectacle, something
beautiful to some watcher,
if watchers there be.

INVISIBLE

Some places in the world everyone believes in ghosts. Shakespeare and Marlowe believed in them, even if only the way dreams are real, as part of life, of being human. Why can't we leave ghosts be, why are we so concerned with delivering them to worlds other than this one? Exorcisms, whisperings, ghost-busting, let them dwell in the backyard where the old house burnt down. Let them float about the woods, or haunt the church belfry, travel in wireless currents like birds migrating, though I've never heard of them drifting in flocks. That's what I'd do if I were a ghost, find other ghosts to fly with, sometimes, for the thrill.

Why be in any hurry to leave? Why not wander through time's windows and distortions, like crossing streets? Perhaps ghosts can view their own lost lives the way actors watch movies in which they star, flawed performances that cannot be changed, long ago released to the world's audiences. Maybe through fissures, cracks in time, ghosts might break a window, turn a clock's arm, make a footprint, but the beauty is in invisibility. It must feel strange when people walk through you, a brief rush, erotic.

I think of the ghost whose favorite haunt is where some company has constructed a strip mall, wandering the plane of the roof like an angel. She closes her eyes and she's back in the meadow again, but cannot tell if it's the future, or her own dreamt past.

SWIFTS AT DUSK

Dog-fighting the invisible, they appear
like the Lafayette Escadrille or Flying Circus.
More hive than flock, swarm of black angels,
out that old giant chimney the swifts pour
like bats out of hell then scatter to soar
off to who knows where.

Fastest of birds, on a strict diet of flying insects,
they cannot perch, so all things but sleep
and brood are done on the wing. Their return
is counter-clockwise clockwork, hundreds of specks
crisscross lower and lower as though

they were weaving a transparent net
while the huge wheel they make turns into
a funnel and they freefall in for the night.

PAGE POND

Wherever you are in the universe
you're at its center, cosmologists say.
My little mutt and I have made
a miraculous journey. Seeking
to chase a hare, flush a woodcock, to hear
a black and white warbler, hiding thrush,
exhaust all worry hiking hard,
we've stirred a flurry of daysleep moths.
We've found ourselves at an angle
where the summer moon is white and blue,
visible well into morning.
We've discovered ourselves at the center
of a universe that happens to be bordered
by cattails and highly annoyed blackbirds.

MERLINS

are moving farther south, arriving here
for our golf courses. They do not build nests
but pilfer crow and blue jay homes. These
little falcons, sky pirates, do not stoop
to conquer, do not scavenge road kill,
but strike in flight, preying on small birds.
They have no fear of humans. The open vistas
of pristine green seem created
to hunt sparrow and starling. To be

a merlin for one day, to eat life raw,
soaring 100 miles per hour, never lighting
on earth. To sleep dreamless all night
in a stolen nest, or, if to dream, dream only
of morning that, unbidden, appears.

MIDNIGHT AT THE 24-HOUR LAUNDROMAT IN CORINTH, NEW YORK

As though below zero meant beneath the sea,
steam has fogged the windows so it's like
we're under water in a submarine
pulsing through winter. Is there a skipper
on board, an invisible insomniac captain
like me, alone in this luminous room
with People Magazine and The Watch Tower?
Without, the Adirondacks loom,
sonar forces immense around the sub.
The engines of the dryers cruise on
while the washers' portals sing song
an ocean's madness. The sub is on chart
through the frozen mountains and beyond
to the infinite sea of stars.

BOATS IN FIELDS

are not uncommon here,
as if farmers in the Taconics
were fishermen or sea captains stranded.
Sea Raven, Flying Fish, Little Magic,
Marylou returned to their
woody birthplaces? But these
are fiberglass. Do the owners imagine
one night, the mist rising in a swell,
their boats cresting away
over blue mountains?
Or is it the abandoned fields
gone to meadow, become ocean,
the land of farmers gone to sea.

WHICH MOUNTAIN

We peered over the high stone wall
behind the little church,
Kathleen McCoy and I, uncertain
which of the twin mountains,
two green icebergs, was Ben Bulben.
And what was the other called, Benwisken
or Tievebawn? We were gazing
in the wrong direction. No matter, we

were more engaged by the birds,
the unrelenting rooks,
a dozen nests or more
in the oaks in the graveyard
where the poet's bones lie, deaf
to their rabble, rude
with life. How strange their raucous
hovering forth and back
over the lyric man's bones. How
difficult their rawness, the call
to make harmony out of
the teeming clouds, the air
that is drinking us.

FABLE

When we first moved near the marsh a neighbor
told me that in the swamp lived a white stag
no hunters could kill. They stalked decades
yet the stag kept elusive, maybe
too quick. The marsh a trackless maze,
maybe he kept to bogs no one could roam.
Hunters kept searching long after the stag
became ghost, if you believe in ghosts.
As if they never existed, those hunters
are dead and gone. The swamp undrained,
impenetrable still. And, on a day when snow
is melting, a heavy mist rises there,
so thick you think anything might appear.

1963

When they paired us with partners
for our year-end sixth-grade dance,
Janet and I were matched. Rehearsals
went fast—she was graceful and sweet.
Both of us shy—I liked holding her hand—
arms around waists, bowing and curtsies—

till the boys down the road began,
Stuie's dancing with a nigger.
We were alone on a bench. Her lips trembled.
Ashamed of my first cowardly act,
I offered to ask teachers to make us exempt.
They refused. We danced I believe better
than everyone else. I don't remember
how to square dance, but I remember her,
Janet, O Janet, pretty and slender.

CATS ASLEEP

Often I have mocked the poets
of the Age of Reason, the Enlightenment
masters of cat poems, Pope,
Swift, Smart, Johnson, Cowper,
but then there is my cat, Walnut, who
of an afternoon, curls up and disappears
into himself. As the great thinkers
of our time claim there is no self,
Walnut, drowsing into oblivion,
goes to the great nowhere
night where stars
originate, where the world is
before language, before the big bang,
where the winds come singing.

GREEN MIDNIGHT

Did I imagine, hear or read somewhere
that if only 3% strove to rescue
the earth for human habitation
they could carry the rest of us through
with all the millions of species we need
who don't need us? I've also been told the Greeks
of Homer's time, the Danaans,
had no word for blue, hence the wine-dark sea,
gray-eyed Athena, and the sky, green?
Maybe on another planet
in another galaxy, the night sky,
not blue-black like ours, but viridescent,
and in that world the color blue is absent
like all the unnamed colors on earth unseen.

✧ III ✧

REDWINGS

FINDING A BLOODSTAIN INSIDE A BOOK OF POEMS

I assume it's mine. After all, who reads
poems, or a book by this forgotten poet.
But what's really odd is, as I roamed
inside, I found the lines, *On finding*
a bloodstain of mine inside a book of poems.
Beneath the stain, an inscription, **The Works**
of Thomas Hood, *To Miss Katie P. Deegan.*
From a friend. September 1st, 1878.

What I was doing that day is lost.
It boils down to two things, maybe.
Either the entire world is possessed
of forms not quite vanished, or, we who feel
such hauntings are mad as the wind at 4 a.m.

WILD HIVE

Inside the tree's womb a choir ruumes from
what seems a miniature power plant, drones

bee song. The ancient pine gurgles. Possessed,
the bearers of perfection shape hexagons

upon hexagons, the bees' idea of infinity. Here
are the cells where the air's invisible runways

are conceived in chambers where thought and song
are fused. Who conducts their hymns,

Gregorians gone mad, fiercely
composing bee-wine. Their oratory churns

electric, mind of guardians, bristled with stingers.
More than the sky, the wind's robots,

they concoct ambrosia for the prophets
that is the same gold as their bodies,

fly like grooms into the flowers and wallow
like messengers gone drunk. Then, propelling body

as compass, return to that aerial cathedral,
that clandestine brain, and with an alchemy

of spittle and pollen create combs soaked
in amber, smelt the earth down to its essence

of honey. Little flyers, little flyers, their chorus
a living waterfall, a wall of rapture and menace.

CRICKETS

$1 a dozen
$4.00   5 dozen

said the sign on the door at Benson's
Pet Supply. I read the sign walking in
for a bag of cat food,
re-read it on my way out and,
on a sudden whim, considered the bargain.
Standing outside, checking my wallet,
I still had a five and wouldn't it be grand
to set them all free
in my garden. But
it was January
and the wind
was ripping hard
with snow
in the forecast
and what
would I do
with 60 crickets
until spring.

CLOUDS

Rain ended with light in the evening sky,
the clouds scattered into pods
of whales, or the ghosts
of Steller's Sea Cows
or alien space craft.
Or those Viking long ships
now coasting overhead,
their gray hulls ominous,
soon to raid the poor villagers
of the towns north and west.
I could warn the good people
of Hebron and Argyle,
but I know
they just won't listen to me.

DISTANCE

Four a.m. I light a candle
and the darkness fractures.
In the bowl on the table
the dead black-eyed Susans
sprout blooms across the walls

as if trying to remember something
in this place so far from summer,
the buried garden,
the visitations of bees.

Here they have overgrown the room
a shadow bouquet
trembling on the walls
as the flowers
ascend the house
toward the field of star clusters
whose blossoms flicker
in the frozen night
like bees.

CASTAWAY

Some winter nights the drifts about the house
become waves
gales blast the walls
the house groans
below the stars and the ocean
of constellations
the deaf antenna is a yardarm
the wooden hulls
hold fast yet there is something

in the shrieking wind
that the house registers
as though the wood recalls
and is trying to sing
back before the creaking masts
sway and they
are something else
moving inside the wind

KALOKALO

24, a stranger in a sweet land of 300 islands,
my hut high on a windy plateau where

I wandered out on nights to watch the stars.
I could recognize the Southern Cross

but did not know that seeming chaos
of the southern constellations was named

for an imaginary ship, Argo
Navis, crewed by people who never were.

I was learning names: *vula*, moon; *waga*, boat;
vuka, flying; *wagavuka*, airplane;

ika, fish; *ikavuka*, flying fish; *kalo*, star;
kalokalo, night sky; *wai*, water;

tui, king; *waitui*, ocean.
One night a glittering constellation

emerged on the sea, a liner, party ship.
I could hear, faintly, disco music.

No one on that ship aware of my watch,
only the captain charting a nearby island

as he wove his vessel through a flower braid
of reefs, and, perhaps, some dreamer,

leaving the party, leaning on the rail,
wondering about that dark mass of an island,

unlit, looming, populated by other dreamers,
who slept as the ship drifted far

into the night as if it never existed
and the unnamed stars remained unnamed.

WINTER WOOD

Gazing through a maze of trees,
tangle of deadfall and life—
for any being who flies or glides,
this wood abides
as a conjuration of labyrinths
where the swiftest exit
is skyward, and nothing needs
to leave but me.

HEARTS

Shelley drowned, body three days at sea, brine
and bloat. His friends built a pyre
but the heart, sea-soaked,
wouldn't burn. Fished from the ashes for Mary,
what became of the keepsake,
desk-bound, paperweight, garden stone?

Thomas Hardy's heart, saved
to be buried with his first wife, Emma,
left upon the kitchen counter in a box,
was pilfered by the family cat,
dragged into a woodlot
and devoured. A heart-shaped stone
will mark the garden border where feral cats
roam this world of twists
and stealth, its concealed havoc.

REDWINGS

We wondered where she'd go, whether
she'd carom off a branch or slam into
someone's windshield, but from her careers

beneath stratus clouds thought her fallen, stunned
somewhere, pondered those who'd rescue her. None

would rouse this one but other blackbirds, who'd coax
her into marshes where they flock in March,

choose new mates each spring. They'd remember her,
a lost sister, while she imprinted on
their songs, morphing back into one of theirs,

forgetting us just as we forget, thriving
in the simple wind. Or she wouldn't. Helpless

like us, they'd keep vigil while she withered,
unable to fathom ailing. We never see

a bird fall from the blue. Eventually
they'd bury her weightless corpse in no one's
backyard, but deep inside the soughing sky.

CITIZEN SPARROWS

Watching citizen sparrows is like
watching humans in pure form
if we could fly, be without sorrow
like open books, without ego.
Sparrows always active in their world
so close to ours, in our eaves and other
unnoticed places, their minor dramas,
their falling providences, as they flit
outside this coffee shop for crumbs we drop.

So much simpler to write about them,
the value of many sparrows who hop
table to table, between legs, dart off
in gangs, then return on some whim or
because something happens we don't see.

LONG TIME

It must have taken a long time of staring
at the stars to make plows and bears, hunters,
goddesses, heroes, sea serpents
and satyrs. Or not.
As a child I gazed into that vastness
and felt, concealed somewhere deep
in that sparkling scape, beings
more than us. It has taken
me a long time to see lions and twins
and teapots in the heavens. To catch
a hint of Andromeda, the chained
beauty, on the verge
of being eaten by a fiend, saved
by a guy on a winged horse.

DOUBLE HELIX

How did Archimedes or Zeno
or Anaximander manage
to configure the endless?
Perhaps they studied the ants,
their astronomical numbers,
the ants who know the earth as infinite,
everything beyond
insubstantial and dream.

How did John Wallis, in 1657,
intuit infinity's shape
related to the DNA molecule?
The ancients would not embrace
the idea of infinity as vague
or random formlessness.
All things must have a shape.
Mountains, mathematics, ocean, stars
suggested infinity. The infinite
must loop around itself
carrying chromosomes like galaxies,
genes like stars.

BLACKBOARD

The blackboard mapped with equations,
seen from an odd angle,
looks like the Homeridae's code,
the saga of an ancient journey
that twists into a map:
Here are giants who eat men; here are islands
of beautiful women, but don't go there;
here is the home of the winds; here the wormhole
leading to the land of the dead.
Not words, but symbols. They describe
a vastness, an infinity
imaginable to no one, archipelagoes
of planets, stars, nebulae, the windy way
back home for which only one route opens.

OFTEN

Shakespeare was wrong about his sonnets.
The image of his love is only
an echo that does not live on, unless
we embody that shadow with our own
still breathing sweetheart.

I could write about the time my love
and I made our first embrace,
but the poem could never freeze the moment,
the naked thrill simply a reflection traced
on paper. Better to write about the birds,

what they were up to that day. Raucous crows
and starlings feeding on scraps we tossed,
the sparrows under the eaves fucking
like crazy, not long, but often.

SYRINX

This morning's yard is warbling wrens, sparrows,
Cardinals, robins, pillaging sky and lawn.
Possessed wrists of delight who draw
The winding air alive with their stitch

And warp. Whatever ornithologists
May think of the riot robins spin,
Or their singing's function, I imagine
It's all just simple joy, a serenade

To being that leaves me thinking maybe
After all we're not alone, and our reason
Here is to hear. Whatever idea
We might cast about being's fate or core

Must pale, its mist structure fading before
The sparrows' weave; their lilt a spell, a code,
A grammar lost in strains each singer knows.

THE HERMIT THRUSH

Rare to see this plain brown bird:
its floating fugue can't be captured.
I've not the dedication of John Clare
twisting on knees through brambles and prickers
to find his way to a nightingale's nest,
the source of a summer warble.
What he found: another dull brown bird,
a homely nest concealed in prickly thorn.
And he, a bit surprised to find such beauty
arising from a creature so unadorned,
somewhat like himself. Nothing's changed.
The hermit sends me homesick for a place
I've never been before, or am going to,
another earth the thrush's song leads through.

NOTES

Syrens and **Syrinx:** Syrinx, ancient Greek for panpipes, the name for the vocal organ of birds, which enables them to sing in multiple voices, creating simultaneous melodies.

Carolina Wrens: Naturalist and author, Dr. Curt Stager is a professor at Paul Smith's College in the Adirondacks. Comparing human vocal chords with those of wrens he said, "We got flutes, wrens got bagpipes."

Ants: Thoreau's description of an ant war is in the "Brute Neighbors" chapter of *Walden*.

Kalokalo: As a Peace Corps volunteer in the Fiji Islands, I lived on the island of Koro. Koro at the time had no electricity, affording clear views of the night sky. Argo Navis was a large constellation in the southern sky that has since been divided into the three constellations of Carina, Puppis, and Vela.

Hearts: Percy Bysshe Shelley's heart was calcified like stone by the sea. Mary Shelley kept the heart in her desk drawer, its whereabouts today unknown. Thomas Hardy's ashes are at Westminster Abbey, something he did not wish for. Hardy, an atheist, wanted his body buried next to second wife, Florence, and his heart buried with or next to his first wife, Emma. There are differing versions as to the fate of the heart, but many endorse the cat version, which I suspect Hardy himself might have liked.

ABOUT THE AUTHOR

STUART BARTOW teaches writing and literature at SUNY Adirondack, and also chairs the Battenkill Conservancy, an environmental non-profit. *His Teaching Trout to Talk: the Zen of Small Stream Fly Fishing,* received the non-fiction award from the Adirondack Center for Writing, and a previous collection of poems, *Einstein's Lawn,* is also published by Dos Madres.

Other books by Stuart Bartow
published by Dos Madres Press

Einstein's Lawn (2015)

He is also included in:
Realms of the Mothers:
The First Decade of Dos Madres Press - 2016

For the full Dos Madres Press catalog:
www.dosmadres.com